on my way home

"Knowing others might benefit from reading her book gave Joyce significant pleasure. She felt this was one last service she could give others. The desire to contribute generously never left her."

From the afterword by **Joyce Rupp**
Catholic writer, speaker, and retreat leader

A Hospice Nurse's Journey
with Terminal Cancer

on my way home

Joyce Hutchison
Coauthor of *May I Walk You Home?*

With a foreword and afterword by
Joyce Rupp

Ave Maria Press AVE Notre Dame, Indiana

Founded in 1865, Ave Maria Press is a ministry of the United States Province of Holy Cross.

www.avemariapress.com

Paperback: ISBN-13 978-1-59471-729-1

E-book: ISBN-13 978-1-59471-730-7

Cover image © iStockphoto.com.

Cover and text design by Katherine Robinson.

Printed and bound in the United States of America.

Library of Congress Cataloging-in-Publication Data is available.

Contents

Foreword
by Joyce Rupp

A late-April rain fell softly the last time I visited Joyce Hutchison. Robins fresh from migration chirped happily in the wet grass. Memories of our friendship washed over me as I walked from the car to her residential building. I buzzed number 106 and moved down the hallway to Joyce's condominium, where she had entered home hospice care more than a month earlier.

The irony of the moment did not escape me. Through the years I often reminded Joyce that she taught me all I knew about death and dying. In addition to my work as a volunteer in the hospice facility where she served as director, Joyce's stories in the grief and loss books we coauthored provided me with valuable insights about end-of-life issues. She had an ease with dying people and an acceptance of death that astounded me. I always thought Joyce would be the one to sit by my deathbed. I never dreamed it would be the other way around.

But there I stood by the door—me, the healthy one—going in to say good-bye to my terminally ill mentor and friend. Even though we knew each other for almost thirty years, the time I shared with her before her death taught me in a most intimate way what it is like to die. Those two and three-quarter years also deepened my love and appreciation for a woman whose heart was wider than anyone's I have ever known.

Joyce's journey opened my eyes to the reality that no matter how much we know about dying, or how often we have accompanied others in their final stage of life, we do not really know what it is like until we face our own mortality. In this book you will find an honest portrayal of an oncology nurse and hospice director who could not sidestep any of the harshness and challenges of her own dying process. Because of how she drew from her vast experience and knowledge to cope with cancer, you will receive encouragement in knowing what to expect and how to respond in a way that lends support for both patient and caregiver.

Throughout her years of coping with cancer, Joyce found herself traversing a lot of medical hills and valleys but never faltered in her belief that God was with her. This faith did not eliminate the physical, emotional, and mental anguish that bled into her experience with cancer. It did give her strength to meet the dreaded aspects of the disease, and she drew forth an ability to live her best qualities, which were many.

When Joyce asked me if I would offer assistance in writing her account of having lung cancer, I had no idea how intimate this accompaniment would be. She allowed me to slip inside the privacy of her relationship with God and to know how terminal cancer affects every tissue of the human experience. I observed the toughness of her journey when I saw her struggle with pain management, physical impairment, and relationship disappointments. I watched how her sparkling eyes and welcoming smile greeted visitors on days when she could hardly manage to stay awake and pain nipped her body with every coughing breath. I heard her laughter in the never-ending sense of humor that was one of her central trademarks and felt the depths of her sorrow when she wept for the heartbreaking medical diagnosis of one of her children.

I witnessed a woman whose expansive heart held room for everyone, especially troubled and ill people; a forgiving person who let go completely of the hurt others knowingly and unknowingly caused; a generous soul who continued to serve others in need and made every effort to do so even though cancer greatly hampered her efforts; a mother and grandmother whose dedicated love for family led her to endure years of tough chemotherapy in order that her life be extended for them.

I observed Joyce's struggle to be the receiver instead of the giver, listened as she described making the significant change from extroverted to introverted prayer, heard her say yes to pain medication she did not want to take, and saw her give in to long hours of rest that felt like defeat to her. (The message from her youth, "Only lazy people stay in bed," left Joyce feeling guilty for having to sleep for such extended periods each day.)

Joyce loved people. She took every opportunity to go to lunch with relatives and friends and attend as many social events as she could manage in her failing health. One time she went with friends to a Christmas luncheon. The next day she told me that all she wanted to do after she arrived there was "to lay my head down on the table and sleep." She fought increasing physical weakness and did her utmost to remain independent even after she became a hospice patient.

Most tender of all was observing how transparent Joyce's spirit became. I watched approaching death transform her into a golden readiness, a humble eagerness to return to the next sphere of life that Joyce named "home."

A friend recently remarked about Joyce, "Her face welcomed you even before you were introduced." That comment fit perfectly. People who met Joyce rarely forgot her, whether they knew her as their oncology nurse, colleague, or acquaintance. She drew each person into her heart with unrestrained kindness.

In his book *Home with God*, the attributes Neale Donald Walsch gives his mother are fitting ones for Joyce Hutchison: "Mom had an unshakable faith that she was stepping into the arms of God. She knew what life was about and she knew what death was not about. Life was about giving all that you had to all that you loved, without hesitation, without question, without limitation. Death was not about anything closing down, but about everything opening up."[1]

Preface

Little did I know I would be writing a third book, this one about facing my own death. My first book, *May I Walk You Home?*, contains twenty-five stories about my hospice patients. I wrote it with the purpose of helping those who care for loved ones in the last stages of life. I followed this publication with a sequel, *Now That You Have Gone Home.* The stories and insights in this book focus on the grief and loss occurring with the death of a loved one.

I hope writing about my experience with terminal cancer will assist those who are also in what I believe to be the most difficult stage of life. Since I was diagnosed with stage-four lung cancer in July 2013, I decided to share how I am traveling this journey because it is one we will all travel eventually. Some of us will move suddenly on this passage and some of us will advance slowly. No matter how long this period of dying takes, I hope you will find kinship and support from *On My Way Home*.

I also hope the insights and experiences gathered in this book will assist others in good health to support and reassure the dying. I've learned so much during these two and a half years as I've faced my own cancer. I realize much more intently what is helpful and what is a hindrance when others interact with someone who is dying. I have also come to a clearer awareness about the reality of what it is like to have a limited time left to live.

Having spent much of my nursing career with people in the last stages of life, I have come to believe death is the natural unfolding of our human lives. I compare the dying process to that of a baby being born. If that child could write a book about coming forth from the womb, we would learn what it is like to emerge into a vastly different existence. We would discover how it is to be suddenly thrust into a brand-new realm. I think we would be amazed at what that child would tell us, how what he or she had feared about birth changed into the sheer amazement at a life the child could never have dreamed possible while in the womb.

That is how I perceive the process of dying. It is as natural to die as it is to be born. Our death births us out of this life into another one we cannot now imagine. I want to assure anyone afraid of dying that we are going to a wonderful place. God is walking with us every step of the way.

Place your hand in God's hand, and do not fear.

Introduction

On April 1, 1940, my mother, Madelyn LaFollette, gave birth to my twin brother, Joe, and me on her birthday. I grew up with two older brothers and one younger on a farm near the rural town of Leon, Iowa. We all went to a one-room country school for nine years of elementary education. I went on from there to graduate in 1958 from Leon High School in a class of seventy-eight students.

Ever since I was about ten years old I wanted to be a nurse. Much of that desire came from my relationship with my grandmother, Grandma Griffin. She was a kind-looking woman with pure white hair that she wore in a bun on the back of her head. Her eyes held so much light, and she always seemed to be smiling. She radiated happiness and became special to me. When she had breast cancer and could no longer care for herself, she came to live with our family the last year of her life.

My mother was depressed and unpleasant with Grandma Griffin most of the time. I asked Grandma a couple of times why Mom was crabby with her, and Grandma would just say, "Your mom has a lot to do with raising five kids and all the work on the farm. She's just tired sometimes. She doesn't mean to be that way."

In spite of how irritable Mom could be with her, Grandma managed to be both fun and funny. I loved to be with her. Before she became too ill to do so, each summer she went to Maloy, Iowa, and stayed with her two bachelor nephews. While there she would cook, clean, and do laundry for them. I usually went with her because I thought it was fun and liked helping her with the work.

Her nephews, Frank and Pat, appreciated having her there. They would talk and reminisce with Grandma. Of course, they loved the wonderful home cooking. They owned a small grocery and a general store in Maloy. There was only a post office and a Catholic church in the town, so everyone hung out at their place. I would go to the store, and they would let me run the cash register. I remember how patient they were with me.

Grandma Griffin developed a recurrence of breast cancer when I was fourteen, and that was when she came to stay at our house. Along with the cancer, she suffered severely from broken bones in her back. My dad tended to be more of a nurse than my mom, who would sometimes become ill when someone around her was sick. Dad used to come in from doing farm work to give Grandma a shot for pain.

My teacher my eighth-grade year did a poor job of instructing, so my mother let me stay home a couple of days a week that year to take care of Grandma Griffin. I liked being able to do that. I would help her with a sponge bath and moisten her forehead with a cool washcloth. I often rubbed lotion on her skin, and I loved to just sit with her. She became so dear to me. She died in April of my eighth-grade year. I felt sad, but I knew she didn't have to suffer anymore. Being the teenager I was, I didn't let myself think too much about her death because I nervously anticipated my move from the one-room country school to a high school of about four hundred students.

The following September my oldest brother, Ed, enlisted in the Air Force and my twin brother, Joe, and I started high school. After I graduated from there I enrolled in Mercy Hospital School of Nursing in September of 1958. I immediately fell in love with nursing, inspired by one of the nuns on the staff who taught us that when we were taking care of our patients, we were taking care of Jesus. That message has always inspired my interactions with my patients.

After I graduated, I worked at Mercy Hospital in the area of orthopedics. There were several elderly patients on this floor, and I thoroughly enjoyed caring for them. Like my Grandma Griffin, the elderly always seemed grateful for the smallest of kindnesses.

A month after I graduated from nursing school, I went home to Leon for the weekend and happened to be at Dairy Queen, where I met Gary Hutchison. Little did I know we would be married less than a year later—we started dating soon after that unexpected encounter and quickly fell in love. Besides being handsome, kind, and gentle, one of Gary's qualities that drew me to him was the way he treated his mother. It was easy to see how much he loved her and how good he was to her. I noticed Gary was thoughtful to his whole family and also kind to mine. My twin brother, Joe, was my best buddy. The two of them soon became best buddies too. Gary had a great sense of humor, and I loved him for that as well.

Gary and I were married ten months later on April 28, 1962. We both wanted children but were told we would be unable to conceive them. What a surprise and joy when I became pregnant and bore our son, Joe, in 1964 and then two more children: Mike in 1965 and Julie in 1967. Besides wanting to be a nurse, I can't remember a time when I did not long to be a mother. I was blessed with my children, and years later, I discovered immense joy in being a grandmother to my nine grandchildren.

It was during that time that I went to work for the oncologist Dr. Tom Buroker. From the time he came to practice in Des Moines, Iowa, in late 1978 until I left the practice for full-time hospice work in 1989, I worked with him. Dr. Buroker is a big man, with a heart as big as his body. His incredible sense of humor and his kindness endeared him to many. When I worked side by side with Dr. Buroker as his oncology nurse for long hours each day, I could say whatever I wanted, and he never seemed to get upset. When you work twelve hours a day for ten years with someone like him there is kind of a sibling bond that develops. He never called anyone by their real name and always called me "Juice."

I would meet him at 6:30 a.m. to accompany him as he made rounds to his patients at the four hospitals. On one of those days we also held an outpatient clinic at Iowa Methodist, then we went back to the hospital for the people who were to be admitted—it was an exhausting day. I walked into my house at 9:30 one evening, and Gary said, "I have dinner in the oven. Go sit down, take your shoes off, and put your feet up." When he came in with the food, he gasped. "You don't have any bottoms in the feet of your hose. They're just strings!" We both laughed and then Gary quipped, "You go back and tell Dr. Buroker tomorrow that he walked your socks off!"

Both Dr. Buroker and his wife, Patty, did many thoughtful and generous things for my family throughout our working relationship. What a gift to know such an incredible, thoughtful, and kind human being. Little did I know during my work with him how much I would need this dear colleague and friend when I began my own fight with cancer.

chapter 1

My Diagnosis

I first began to face the reality of my impending death in April 2013. I had just recovered from a hip replacement two months earlier when I developed a cold and a nagging cough. I didn't feel too bad. After the surgery I was walking on my own again and excited to not have any pain. I didn't want "a little cold" to slow me down, so I never gave it a second thought. When Gary became sick with cancer, I went to work full-time; plus I had to be there for the three children. I learned to just keep going when I did not feel well. I became good at ignoring sickness or not recognizing when I was ill, but this resiliency did not serve me well when it came to the persistent cough.

At my first appointment with my primary physician in April, he told me the cough was due to allergies. I was looking forward to an upcoming trip to attend a conference in Florida, so even though I was not feeling well I went ahead and flew there. While at the conference, I felt progressively worse. I barely had enough energy and breath to walk to the airport gate for my return home.

The next day I returned to the doctor, who now told me I had a problem with my heart. Following that visit, I was admitted to the coronary intensive care unit (CICU), and a tube was inserted into my pericardium. I was hooked to suction for forty-eight hours. The pericardium is the sac around the heart, and mine was full of fluid. This was squeezing on my heart, causing a condition called cardiac tamponade. Almost a pint of fluid was removed. After four days, I was transferred to the medical floor of the hospital. Two days later they discharged me with a diagnosis of pneumonia and switched me from IV to oral antibiotics.

In spite of knowing that information, I continued to be in a state of denial. I knew that tamponade was associated with cancer—if the fluid is bloody, it is a strong indication of cancer. But I somehow blocked out that possibility. I look back now and believe that, unconsciously, I was growing more and more fearful. As an oncology nurse I used to wonder how people could be in denial and ignore blatant signs of cancer. Now I know. Looking back, I cannot imagine how I did not question it because every sign spelled cancer. I do wonder how the doctors could have missed it too. Perhaps denial was the only way for me to have time to absorb the truth of my physical condition.

During that time, cancer was briefly mentioned by medical personnel and then ruled out. Now that I look back, I am truly disgusted that I did not advocate for myself and request a pulmonary referral. I just didn't feel bad enough to think I could have cancer—in hindsight it couldn't have been clearer. I stayed on those oral antibiotics for more than a week and went to my physician again. This time she told me it looked like I had tuberculosis. She then called a few days later to say I did not have it. That was no surprise. I knew I did not have TB. I felt angry, impatient, and more realistic. At this point, I asked to see a lung specialist.

A week later I saw Dr. Hicklin. He put me on a third antibiotic and asked me to come back in two weeks or so, which really concerned me. I thought, *Two weeks? Why so long when I keep getting worse?* At the end of a week, I called for an earlier appointment because I was coughing almost continually and getting more short of breath. It had now been *more than two months* since I started trying to get relief from my persistent cough.

At the appointment, Dr. Hicklin performed a thoracentesis to check for fluid around the lungs. A long needle was inserted between two of my ribs and about a quart of fluid was taken from around the lung, and I could breathe better after that. Then the fluid was sent to the lab for pathology testing. That afternoon I went to the hospital for a bronchoscopy, in which a biopsy was taken of a mass that was found in my lung. Dr. Hicklin assured me he would call the next day with the results of the bronchoscopy.

The next day about noon, even though he was out of town in Chicago, Dr. Hicklin called to say, "I am sorry to tell you that you have lung cancer—adenocarcinoma of the lung. I am going to call Dr. Buroker right away."

I felt comforted by that because of my long relationship with Dr. Buroker. He called me within twenty minutes after Dr. Hicklin notified him and asked me to come to his office at 4:00 p.m. that same day.

My mind swirled for the three hours prior to going to see Dr. Buroker. *I surely can be cured—after all, I have worked in oncology, hospice, and palliative care for thirty-five years. It makes no sense for me to have cancer—especially terminal cancer.* I felt numb and unable to get one thought straight. I asked myself, *What is going on?* I thought of the people I cared for all those years and had given chemotherapy. They were so sick. I remembered that the ones with lung cancer often died. My memories of caring for those people made me feel scared and vulnerable. Then my mind would dismiss those thoughts and go to, *This is just a small thing. It won't amount to much.*

When I went for my visit, Dr. Buroker gave me a big hug. I felt bad for him. I could tell it was hard for him to get the news about my condition. I knew he would be concerned for me, and I didn't want him to have to go through that. At the same time, I wanted him to be my oncologist. I trusted him completely. He explained the pathology report and added that we would need to get more tests to know what we were dealing with. He would order blood tests, a brain scan, and a PET scan to make sure it hadn't gone to the liver, bones, or brain. Dr. Buroker gave me hope, saying that there was currently a pill out that did not have side effects. With this pill, there was a 60 percent chance I could live five years.

My reaction at that possibility surprised me. I thought, *Gee, five years isn't very long.* A blood test would indicate the results, and I didn't ask him what the prognosis was if I didn't qualify for the pill and had to go on chemotherapy because I was afraid of the answer. He was so kind and assured me, "We are going to do everything to whip this, Juice."

The new pill seemed to be amazing and hopeful. Yet why did five years seem so short? Was I just being greedy? I thought, *Dear God, my only hope is five years. That doesn't seem like nearly enough time. I feel helpless. My granddaughters Margaret and Anabel will still be in high school. The other grandchildren will still be young too.*

I received all my appointments for the scans and tests. Then I left. Again, it kind of felt as if I were watching all this happen to someone else. It just couldn't be me. I love and trust God so much. I don't fear dying, but I thought I would live a much longer life.

chapter 2

Telling My Children

I must tell my children. The thought of letting them know brought immediate heartache and added to my difficulty of accepting the diagnosis. They, of course, knew I was having some health issues because of my hospital stay two months earlier. I will never forget the day I had to call and tell them about my cancer.

First I spoke with Mike because he lives near me in Des Moines. I always think of him as a gentle giant because he physically appears strong and yet has such a soft heart. Mike had been extremely distraught when I was in the CICU. I felt the news of my cancer would be even more difficult for him. Mike and I have a close relationship. For the last fifteen years he's lived in Des Moines, and we have become used to helping one another. When Mike's dad, my husband Gary, died, Mike lived a great distance away in Atlanta, Georgia. Nevertheless, he came back to visit me every four to six weeks during the first year after Gary's death. It broke my heart to have to call this dear son of mine. When I phoned and told him about the diagnosis, I could tell he was immediately shocked and brokenhearted.

I tried to lessen his hurt by assuring him that I was seeing Dr. Buroker that afternoon and would call as soon as I was finished. Mike could hardly talk, but he tried to be brave and asked, "Do you want me to go with you?" "No," I said, "I won't really find out much, except be scheduled for tests." I knew he wanted and needed to be with me so I suggested, "I'd love for you to go with me when I get the results of the tests."

When her children are sad or unhappy, it breaks a mother's heart. I have always believed we are only as happy as our saddest child. I desperately wanted to protect all my children from a broken heart, but I was helpless to do so. They each went through such deep sorrow when their dad died nineteen years ago. I didn't want them to have to go through that sorrow again.

I kept wondering how Mike would share the news with his sons, fourteen-year-old Griffin and twelve-year-old Garrett. I have a loving relationship with these grandsons. They came to the hospital several months earlier to see me when I was having tests. At that time, Garrett crawled onto the bed beside me and sobbed. Griffin looked desolate and scared. All the tubes and beeps of the CICU must have been frightening. I tried to assure my grandsons that the doctors were going to help me get well soon.

When I called my only daughter, Julie, in Kansas City, Missouri, to tell her about my diagnosis, she responded much like Mike did—instantly upset but attempting to be brave. Julie and I have always had a close relationship, so much so that when her college roommate moved home, Julie wanted me to come and stay with her in the dorm for a few days. We have always been able to talk easily with each other about almost everything. We call each other every day. Julie is married with three children and works as a nurse in pediatrics. She drove to Des Moines and stayed with me while I was in the CICU and gave me a lot of nurturing. I could tell she was just as scared as Mike. I sensed her worry all along, but I didn't think I was sick enough for my situation to be so serious. After I gave Julie the bad news she immediately wanted to come from Kansas City, three hours away. I responded, "Please, don't come yet. We won't know anything for a while."

Julie's three children are sixteen, fourteen, and eleven. I knew they would also be distraught because I am as closely bonded to them as I am to Garrett and Griffin. When Julie's children came to visit me in the CICU, they were sad and concerned. They had never seen me that sick before, and it was frightening for them.

After talking to Julie, I called Joe, who lives in Lynchburg, Virginia. He has always been the one who doesn't show much feeling; he has been the one to be concerned about everyone else—a trait of being the oldest child. Joe is an ENT surgeon. He didn't voice as much emotional response as my other two children because of his years of masking his feelings with patients. Instead, he sounded professional, asking questions. Joe had previously spoken with my other physicians when I was in the hospital, so he might not have been quite as shocked as my other two children were. He probably sensed the severity of my symptoms.

I knew Joe was obviously worried when he suggested, "I'll travel to Iowa to be with you." But I also asked him to wait until we had more information. Again, as a mother, I wanted to protect my children.

Joe has a family—four children, ages eleven to sixteen—plus a busy medical practice. I assured Joe that I would keep him posted. I knew Dr. Buroker well enough to know that he would do the same for Joe.

After I contacted all three children with the news of my cancer, I kept asking myself, *How is this happening to me and my family? I don't want to bring this pain to my children. After all, I have always tried to help resolve it when something difficult was going on with them. Now I am the one being the cause of their pain. They have already been through the loss of their dad when they were young. Isn't this too much?*

My thoughts continued, *I have so much ahead of me. I want to be the best grandma I can be to my grandchildren. What happens to my plans to do volunteer work, especially with palliative care talks and hospice work? This just can't be happening to me. What if I don't get to go to Emma's graduation or any of the other grandchildren's graduations or weddings?*

Then my thoughts went toward Julie. Concerns filled my mind. *How could I possibly leave her when she has teenagers and needs me as a sounding board? I want to be there for her when she needs to air her challenges and frustrations.* My heart beat faster and I pleaded, *Please, God, if possible, let me live a long time. I am not afraid to die, and I look forward to eternity someday, but*

my family needs me now. Please let me live awhile longer.
I also pray my children and grandchildren will be okay.

chapter 3

My Chemotherapy Treatments

After I had all the tests and scans Dr. Buroker ordered, I went back to get the results. I learned that the cancer was in the right lung. It had also spread to the lymph nodes and around the mediastinum, the membranous partition between the lungs. Because the cancer had grown outside of the lung, surgery was not an option, nor was radiation. The other bad news was that I didn't qualify for the pill that Dr. Buroker told me could possibly extend my life five years. That left chemotherapy as the only option for treatment.

I asked about my prognosis after receiving chemotherapy when Dr. Buroker and I were alone. I didn't want my family to know what he would tell me. He looked at me and said, "A year, maybe longer."

I wished I had not asked. My stomach lurched, and my mind questioned, *How can this be?* Dr. Buroker saw the shock on my face, so he added, "But we're going to fight this cancer as hard as we can and see if we can beat it, Juice."

I was to come the next day for chemo because they first had to get it approved by the insurance company. The intravenous chemotherapy treatment would take five hours. I felt frightened and overwhelmed. How could this be happening? I had always been on the other side of cancer, taking care of patients, not the one to *be* the patient.

My husband Gary passed away nineteen years before my cancer diagnosis, and by this time I had remarried. My second husband, Dick, had come with me to the appointment where I received the results of my tests and scans. On the way home Dick commented, "Judy [his first wife] didn't receive any treatments and died in two months. I can't imagine what this is going to entail." His comment sounded like he'd rather I did it like Judy, so we would know what to expect. Then he wouldn't have to witness any prolonged and traumatic illness that I might experience.

Even though Dick made that comment, I knew I could not consider the alternative of foregoing chemotherapy because that meant giving up all hope. I felt I had to fight for my family, including Dick. I thought that surely he would be relieved if he saw that chemo gave me more time. Still, my decision was distressful. I knew the chemotherapy drug combination of cisplatin, Avastin, and Alimta was a tough treatment with strong side effects, including extreme fatigue, constant nausea, and possible vomiting. If this happened then I would also have to be given medication to help alleviate those symptoms, and then those could have side effects.

When I went for the first chemo treatment on August 1, 2013, I was put in a room where I would remain in bed for five hours. Dick, my son Mike, and my grandson Garrett came with me. Dick stayed about two hours and then left to take care of errands. I wasn't surprised because it seemed like he did not want to be there. Before Dick left, I suggested that Mike bring me home afterward. Dick readily agreed.

After he left, Garrett crawled in bed beside me. We talked about how what I was going through with the chemo would help make me better. Garrett was now going to a Catholic school, and I taught him the Our Father that afternoon. He was so excited and prayed the entire prayer for me before he left. We had such a good sharing that day and grew closer as we lay there together during my first chemotherapy treatment.

The next few days were full of every emotion I could experience. Questions of all sorts kept coming. *Oh, my gosh, I have lung cancer that has spread. I wonder if that makes it a stage four? Most patients I took care of with Dr. Buroker died after this diagnosis. How long will I live? Can I protect my children and grandchildren from the pain of it? What is ahead for all of us?*

Besides the emotional and mental turmoil, I was dreadfully sick from the chemo. All I could compare it to was having the most horrific flu possible. I had absolutely no energy. I felt as if the last of my energy had deserted me completely. I found this especially difficult because I always had a ton of energy. But I kept trying to reassure myself. *This isn't too bad because it's going to kill those cancer cells.* I knew it was important to stay positive for myself and everyone around me. I also relied greatly on my dear friend, Jesus. I asked him every morning to walk the day with me. What a great reassurance to know he was there.

My friends were good about calling and bringing food. They were genuinely concerned. Those kindnesses meant more than I ever could have imagined. My children offered continual attention with their phone calls and visits. Joe flew in from Virginia, and Julie and her family frequently came from Kansas City. Mike stopped by several times a week for short stays and wanted to do anything he could. The grandchildren's visits comforted me too. I appreciated all the love and attention I received, even though I felt horribly sick.

As a mother, I felt a bit strange having my kids wait on me hand and foot when I had always been the caregiver and cook. I did everything I could for them when they came to visit, and now here they were doing those things for me. Their love brought me a huge amount of comfort.

During that period I received four courses of the same exhausting chemotherapy treatment every three weeks, a total of almost four months. Just when I didn't think I could be any sicker, I became even more so after each treatment. After the second treatment I ended up in the hospital with low blood counts and sepsis. Another time I passed out from dehydration and was again hospitalized.

In spite of this, I wanted to continue the treatments because I knew they had the best chance of destroying the cancer cells. The vomiting became constant—morning, noon, and night. I spent a lot of time in the bathroom and became terribly weak. Some days I could hardly walk from the bedroom to the family room or bathroom. Consuming food presented a problem too. Although I did not have an appetite, I kept trying to eat fruits and vegetables each day because I knew the importance of keeping up with nutrition. Sometimes strawberry milkshakes tasted the best and were all my body would tolerate. I also tried to drink enough fluids so I would not become dehydrated.

I would just start to feel a bit better, maybe for a few days to a week, when the time to receive chemo would come around again. There were days when I wondered how much sicker I could get and if I would survive it. The weakness eventually became so bad that it didn't even help to ease it by sitting in my chair or lying down. My bones hurt, and I often had a dull headache. Eventually, we realized that Zofran, the nausea medication, was causing the headaches. Once this medication was changed to Compazine, the headaches stopped, and that was a great relief. I discovered that if I took this medicine just prior to bedtime, I could sleep better with no nausea or vomiting during the night. This eased my physical distress significantly.

Eventually, the scans showed some shrinkage of the tumors. That was encouraging. After four courses of treatment, Dr. Buroker said I couldn't have any more cisplatin, the chemo I had been given, because it had worn my body down so much. He said, "If you continue on this, you will end up bedridden and probably be too weak to walk again." Once more, I thought about all the people to whom I had given these drugs. I had no idea they felt that bad or that it affected them in such a drastic way. I really spent a lot of time reflecting on the patients I cared for and how I thought I knew what they were feeling. I assure you, until you are walking the path of cancer yourself, it is impossible to know what it is like.

As I reflected further on my life as an oncology nurse, I hoped that I had been kind to each patient because I now knew the importance of that kindness—to have someone listen without thinking I was a wimp. No one has ever indicated that I am; still, I have not wanted to say how I feel sometimes for fear of coming across as a complainer. Sometimes I just can't help but acknowledge how awful I feel. I hope my patients expressed their true feelings to me when they felt like it and that I was attentive to them. Remembering the experience of my patients led me to wonder, *How will this turn out for me? Am I going to live this way very long and am I going to be this sick the whole time until I die? What is ahead?*

My children were constant cheerleaders. They kept saying, "You can do it, Mom. You are strong."

This gave me more determination and encouragement to continue the difficult treatments. Mike went with me to every appointment. At each one he told Dr. Buroker, "She is strong. She can take another treatment." Those cheers from all three adult children made me want to fight harder. I felt like they were fighting right along with me.

chapter 4

Cancer Affects My Marriage

A diagnosis of incurable cancer can certainly change one's entire life. Little did I know how true this would be in regard to my marriage. At the time I was diagnosed with cancer, I had been married for seven years to Dick, who went to the same high school in southern Iowa that I did. We found each other again at a fiftieth high school reunion and learned that both of our spouses had died. We discovered an attraction for one another and married a year later. Neither of us knew what a challenging relationship our marriage would be.

Only some months after our wedding did we learn how differently we understood what marriage meant. We knew so little about one another's attitudes and lifestyles. I grew to realize that marrying someone when you have adult children and have had a certain way of life for many years is very different from marrying when you are young and have no children.

My husband was used to having a stay-at-home wife who was always available to be with him wherever he went and whatever he did. He expected this of me too, but I had worked full-time ever since I was required to do so at age twenty-nine when my first husband, Gary, became ill with cancer. At that time we had three small children. Gary's health situation consisted of a constant roller coaster of medical complications and life-threatening situations until he died twenty-four years later. After his diagnosis of cancer in 1970, ten years went by before Gary was able to go back to work. That led me to take over as the breadwinner for the family. I was used to responsibilities and activities that extended far beyond the home.

During those years of Gary's illness, I became active in oncology and hospice nursing. Gary and I assisted in starting the first hospice program in Des Moines in 1978. That took up much of my life, but I also stayed involved with my children's school lives. Even though their dad was often sick, I didn't want them to feel less for it and not have a parent there for them. I volunteered to be homeroom mother at school for one of the children each year and became a Little League mom. No matter how busy I was with work, I took them to all their extracurricular activities.

Even though my work required a great deal of energy and my attempts to be there for my children took up a good portion of any other time of mine, I still made sure that home was where they could find a warm meal on the table every evening. Besides all these family responsibilities, I also volunteered at church, especially after the children went to college. When Gary died in 1994, I became active with a book club, a widow's support group, and a hospice caregiver group. I wanted to keep a positive attitude and make a difference in life.

All these activities led me to be a very different marriage partner from Dick's first wife. He expected me to be home all the time and available to go with him when he went to the store or any other place. He and his wife did everything together, while Gary and I planned what we would do together. We enjoyed being with each other, but we also had other separate activities. Because our history was radically different, it's not surprising that Dick and I faced some major obstacles after we married at the ages of sixty-seven and sixty-eight.

Dick became increasingly irritated when my children and friends stopped by. The phone rang frequently. He felt the visits and phone calls took me away from him, and he found it difficult to adjust to not being the sole focus of my attention. After my cancer diagnosis, my friends came even more often, bringing food and doing kindnesses however they could. This situation added to his negative feelings because he again felt they came between us.

This was a whole new journey for Dick. I had three children whom I loved very much and nine grandchildren who were close to me. I thought I understood these differences and believed we could work through them. But I did not fully realize the extreme difficulty Dick was having until he announced in October 2013, five months after I was diagnosed with lung cancer, that he wanted out of the marriage. He probably wondered where he fit in, and I feel bad if that was the case. I was just too sick to continue to work on the marriage. The tension was too great for me to do anything other than accept his decision. Dealing with cancer was all I could manage. I felt I could fight only one major conflict at a time. And so, much to my sadness, the marriage dissolved, adding another loss to my life.

It was a no-win situation. I wish we could have made it work, and I believe in my heart that we both continue to wish we had done so.

As the marriage grew in difficulty and moved toward divorce, I needed to find a more peaceful environment. I knew the added stress in our relationship could hinder my attempts to conquer the dreadful illness I had. When you know your marriage is over and you are trying to live together, even with the best of efforts, life is not pleasant. My husband resisted leaving our house. He insisted he had nowhere else to go. Even though I was the one with cancer, his insistence on staying meant I had to find another place to live.

Mike and Julie spent a huge amount of their time searching for a suitable home for me. After much hunting, Julie called Mike one day and said, "I found one on the Internet that looks like a good option. It's on Grand Avenue. Would you go and look at it?" At the first opportunity, Mike went to check it out. Soon after, he called Julie with excitement about the find, saying, "I think it's just perfect for Mom. It needs a lot of work, but it's a double condo. It's so big that we can all live with Mom when the time comes."

When I felt better and had a decent week with fewer side effects from chemo, Mike brought me over to see the place. I thought it was acceptable, but the space seemed much too large. After more conversation with the children, we decided it really was the one for me and bought it. Because Dick was remaining in our house until it sold, I moved into the condo with only a chair, ottoman, television, and a mattress with box springs on the living-room floor. I sat down in the chair on that first night and couldn't believe how peaceful I felt. The divorce was final. I could live in a lovely place without being stressed by a tense relationship. I didn't care if the place had almost nothing in it. It is strange how we perceive things. I was so relieved to not be in such tense surroundings, I felt like I was living in a palace with all kinds of furniture. My new home was quiet and serene. I didn't have to live in dread of the next disagreement.

Sometimes I had felt like saying, "Couldn't you have waited to be rid of me because I am going to die anyway?" But at the same time, I also remembered how difficult it is to have a peaceful marriage when one spouse is ill. Gary and I had lots of years of love to go on before he had cancer. Even then, his illness sometimes brought difficulties we had to face in our healthy marriage. But we were always able to come to understanding and agreement. That never happened with my second husband.

The day I moved to a place of my own, a huge weight lifted from my heart. I could sense a strength to deal with the cancer that I had not felt since I was first diagnosed.

chapter 5

My Summer
without Chemotherapy

Springtime has come. I have been dealing with chemotherapy for ten months. The recent CT scan showed some shrinkage of the tumor in my right lung. This is good news, and I am encouraged to know the chemotherapy is working. Ever since I was diagnosed, I decided I did not want my entire life to be taken over by cancer. I have tried to go to lunch with my friends, stay active in Stephen Ministry, and be attentive to my other commitments, but I had no idea what it meant to have everything I do become an enormous effort. Even going to the grocery store takes an unbelievable amount of exertion.

I try to run my vacuum sweeper, and I am exhausted in just a few minutes. I would love to drive to Julie's in Kansas City and spend time with her. I've driven the three hours there a couple of times, but I am dog-tired when I arrive. It's discouraging. All I did was drive the car. I did not put forth one bit of work, and I'm still worn out. How could someone be so short of stamina?

When I attend my grandson Garrett's football or basketball games, I sometimes wonder if I will be able to sit on the bleachers for the whole game when my body, especially my legs and back, is so tired. How could my body have become this beaten down? How can just one little activity wear me out completely?

My present condition makes me question my quality of life. I have always been extremely active. I never dreamed I could be this depleted of energy. I do not want to sit in my chair all the time, but lately that is what my days have become. Am I going to spend the rest of my life doing one little thing each day and then taking the rest of the day to recover from that small activity? It's difficult not to get discouraged.

When I next go for my regular appointment with Dr. Buroker, another CT scan is ordered to see where we are with the chemo accomplishing its goal of decreasing the tumor in my right lung and around my mediastinum. Dr. Buroker surprises me by saying, "The tumor has shrunk some more, but it isn't gone. I believe we should stop chemo for a while and give your body a rest." He assures me that they will do a CT scan as frequently as they need to in order to keep track of the size of the tumor. As soon as it starts to grow again, they will put me back on the chemo regimen. He emphasizes, "The most important thing right now is to give your body time to recover. Your body has been beaten up by the chemo you've had."

I am thrilled to stop chemo because I've felt so worn down. At the same time, I wonder what will happen with the tumor. When I am receiving the chemotherapy, it's a constant reminder that some effort is being made to control the cancer. I can imagine the cancer cells being killed every time I get a treatment. When I feel physically drained, I trust it means the chemotherapy is working.

I'm scared to end the treatments, even though I'm also relieved at the same time. I explain this to Dr. Buroker, how happy I am about going off the chemotherapy and, at the same time, questioning if we are taking a risk in doing so. He reassures me we are taking a greater risk at continuing the treatments when my body is so worn out.

He then explains, "The more chemo you have, the longer it takes for your white blood cells and your platelet cells to recover each month." He reminds me that I had to have a blood transfusion recently because my hemoglobin had dropped to almost eight, when it should be twelve to fourteen.

I'm still hesitant about not receiving chemo, but Dr. Buroker assures me he will watch my situation closely. I leave the office both pleased and anxious. We have had good luck shrinking the tumor, and I don't want it to get out of hand. I do have a lot of confidence in Dr. Buroker. I believe he would only do what is the very best for me.

As I am on my way home I think, *The good thing, too, is that it is now the month of May. Maybe I won't have to have chemotherapy all summer. What a nice thing that would be. I could enjoy my grandchildren and their activities. I could go to Kansas City once in a while, maybe even make a trip to Virginia to see Joe, Annmarie, and the grandchildren when I get stronger.*

I come home excited, a little scared, and yet knowing I have the best doctor. He would never do anything to jeopardize my recovery.

As it turned out, I did get to have that entire summer free from chemo. What a blessed reprieve that was for me.

chapter 6

Preparing for My Journey

Let me share my spiritual journey through the past ten months. I have always relied on God for everything. I've continually asked him to walk with me from the time I was a little girl until now. When Gary was sick, I would ask God to be with us through that difficult time. I have no doubt that this divine companion took care of us every step of the way. Then in August, when I found out I had non-small cell cancer of the lung and maybe had a year or more to live, I had to really give thought to where I was spiritually. What did I believe? Where was my hope?

I have known for some time that I am not afraid to die. I truly believe that we will all be going to a wonderful place of love and happiness. Gary taught me that when he had a near-death experience in 1970.

He described how he saw where he was going and there was nothing but absolute love. He had always been a perfectionist and worried a lot. He said, "Where we are going, there is nothing to worry about. I felt perfect love from head to foot." Gary went on to live twenty-four more years. After that experience he remained peaceful about his future death. He would often say, "I want to live a long time, be a grandpa, and grow old with you, Joyce. At the same time, I look forward to where we are all going in the next life. When it's my time, let me go because I will be ready."

I ask myself, *Am I ready?* I believed I was until I received the diagnosis of cancer, but now I am thinking that I don't want to go yet. My children are in their forties and their children are still young, from ages eleven to fifteen. It just doesn't seem right that I would leave them now. *Maybe just a few more years*, I tell myself.

After sitting with those thoughts, I then asked myself, *When will I be ready?* I prayed a lot and meditated on this question and did not find an answer for some time. I truly have no fear of dying because of my work with hospice for more than thirty years. During that time I had to come to grips with any fears I had about dying. I believe we are all on a journey. We come into this world crying, as we begin an unknown future. When our life on this earth is over we are born into the joy of eternal life.

People often say to me, "This isn't fair that you have cancer. You have taken care of so many people through the years in your work with oncology and hospice. This shouldn't be happening to you." That isn't how I feel. It isn't unfair that I have it—no one deserves cancer. After much prayer and reflection on my life and current situation, I have come to a peaceful place.

I don't know how long my life on this earth will be. There is no use in guessing. It is not in my hands. What *is* in my hands is the ability and choice to keep as close to God as possible, to live each day as best I can, and to not give too much thought to how many days, weeks, or months I have left. I will never know how much longer I have—if I spend all the time I have left regretting that I might not have long to live, or being afraid that I won't be here in six months, then I will have missed what today holds for me. In fact, in some ways it is a blessing to face my death because I look at my life a bit differently. There is certainly no need to worry about the little things that happen each day. They come and go. So be it.

Having written that, I admit that I am still a bit of a worrier. I want the lives of my children and grandchildren to be untroubled and free of pain. I am realizing I have very little control over that part of life as well. I am learning to trust God to take care of them.

If I am honest, I admit part of me also wants to live a long time. On the other hand, I don't want to live until I am a burden to my family. I know from my hospice nursing that caregivers learn a great deal as they tend for those they love. I don't want to take that experience away from my family. I have been privileged to care for those who were dying for many years, and those experiences were some of my greatest blessings. Again, I have to remind myself that even this is not in my hands. I don't know what God has in store for any of us, but I trust he will be with us every step of the way. I am leaving my life in his hands.

A friend gave me the book *Jesus Calling* by Sarah Young, which has been a great support to me. Jesus reminds us in daily meditations that he is walking with us and available at any time. What more could I ask?

On one of the days of particular reassurance Jesus said to me through the meditation, "Rest in my radiant presence. The world around you seems to spin faster and faster, till everything is a blur. Yet there is a cushion of calm at the center of your life, where you live in union with me. Return to this soothing center as often as you can, for this is where you are energized: filled with my love, joy, and peace."[1]

Those words brought me immense peace and a sense of security. I can continue with what is ahead, no matter how difficult it might become.

chapter 7

My Chemo Fatigue

After my chemotherapy treatments, I would feel weak in every part of my body. It took a huge effort to put one foot in front of the other. I truly had no idea of the enormity of the fatigue associated with chemotherapy even though Gary used to try to describe it to me. He would say, "It's much worse than the nastiest flu you've ever had." Now I find myself in that exact situation, and I finally understand. It is an effort for me to simply sit on the recliner with my feet up. At times I can't sink far enough into the chair in order to have my body feel rested and not drained totally of energy.

When Gary received chemotherapy more than thirty years ago, the available treatments were not nearly as potent as the kind now available. Even so, the chemotherapy he received constantly drained him of energy. He told me, "When I mention to people that the chemotherapy makes me really tired, they compare it to the kind of fatigue that flu causes. I wish it were that kind of tiredness, but it's much worse. I feel wiped out all the time, and my legs ache with a weariness that's hard to describe."

I thought I understood him, but now I realize that I didn't. I do hope I was as sympathetic as I could be with Gary. I certainly understand what he was talking about now that I have experienced that same sort of thing. There are no words to adequately describe the tiredness. For a few days after the chemo, I just feel terrible all over. I sleep a lot and need to take a considerable amount of medication for the pain. Even after the worst side effects wear off, the exhaustion never leaves. Everything I try to do takes such great effort. I never thought receiving chemo could be this bad.

I learned from receiving chemo how difficult it is to wake each morning and know it will be another day like the day before, with nausea, frequent vomiting, extreme exhaustion, and no appetite. Yet I wanted to live badly enough that I wanted to continue the treatments. During that first tough treatment of chemo I didn't get dispirited very often, but there were definitely days when I questioned the quality of my life. My children and grandchildren remained comforting and encouraging supporters, which helped me endure the treatments. How much I welcomed their affirming words of love.

Sometimes, when I am sitting in my chair after I have been out, I can hardly move. I'm totally bushed. My legs feel "achy tired." Sitting in my easy chair doesn't relieve anything, even though it feels good to sit down. The tiredness makes me so miserable; I can't sit deep enough or sink far enough into the chair to relieve it. The fatigue never leaves.

I also developed neuropathy soon after I started chemotherapy. This affects the nerve endings and results in numbness of the hands and feet. My feet and toes feel numb and tingly. When I'm walking, I can stumble easily if it's a day when I lose sensation in my feet. When I first started experiencing neuropathy, my feet felt like they were asleep. Then it went to a burning feeling. These symptoms are better or worse depending on the type of chemo I am receiving. At times it feels like my feet are bound with bandages even though they have nothing on them. At other times I can hardly feel my feet at all. The same kinds of things happen with my hands, especially the tips of my fingers. I sense them going from numbness to burning to not feeling at all. When my hands are like this, it can be difficult to write, using either my computer or a pen. One day when I was ironing, I burned my hand rather badly because I did not feel the heat of the iron on it.

These days the weariness has found a permanent home deep in my bones. Distractions help. For instance, when I am at lunch with others or talking to someone at my house while I'm sitting in my chair, I don't notice the fatigue so much. But the minute my mind is quiet or I am not involved in something outside of myself, there the tiredness is again, refusing to let me forget about it.

I find myself saying, "I am so tired of being tired." It is really wearing to feel this exhaustion all the time. Maybe it is the aching that goes with it that makes it seem worse than usual. I will be sitting out by the swimming pool, watching my grandchildren swim, and I will think to myself, *I wish the tiredness in my legs would go away*. The warm sun on my legs helps to alleviate it a bit. It also seems like it is partially restlessness in my legs that is bothersome. I want to move them just to get relief. It isn't just in my legs though. My whole body feels like it could fall apart. Everything is an effort. Sometimes getting out of my chair to get a glass of water takes more effort than quenching my thirst is worth.

Everything I have always taken for granted is an effort. I often think, *I just wish I could be free of this long enough to remember what it feels like to have energy.* There are brief moments when I do momentarily feel a bit of vigor: when I am sleeping and the phone rings and wakes me up or I spontaneously awaken in the morning after sleeping all night. For a brief time my body does not have that tiredness. I love this feeling, but it quickly ends. Soon after I get up, my unwanted companion, the dreaded fatigue, returns.

As I write this I feel like I have done a lot of complaining. This may sound like a negative chapter, but it's not meant to be. You truly cannot understand the side effects of chemotherapy unless you experience them. While I describe the difficult side effects from the treatments, I also want to say I am grateful such a variety of excellent chemotherapy drugs exists now. Medicine is doing great things to slow down or stop the growth of cancer.

chapter 8

My Emotional Roller Coaster

At the end of December 2014, a year and a half after my initial diagnosis, I coughed more and experienced shortness of breath. I couldn't help wonder what was going on. I was receiving a weekly chemotherapy treatment of Gemzar and then seeing Dr. Buroker every three weeks. On the last day of December I received my sixth treatment. Dr. Buroker thought my lungs sounded okay but ordered a CT scan for my next visit in January.

I went back and forth about my condition. I would decide my worsening cough was all in my head and I was doing okay. But when I let myself be realistic, I knew my coughing was worsening. I also knew that to walk from my chair to the front door left me wheezing and gasping for breath. Mike assured me I was doing fine, that he didn't notice my increased coughing. But then Julie would tell me the opposite—that she thought my symptoms indicated a declining condition. I leaned more toward believing Julie's opinion because of her nursing background. Mike has a tendency to not want to think about the cancer progressing. Julie doesn't want to see this either, but she can't ignore signals that indicate the change.

When I went to see Dr. Buroker on January 13 after lab work and a CT scan of my chest, he called me into his office. When he showed the last scan alongside the new one, it became evident that the cancer had grown during the time I was receiving Gemzar. The shadow in the biopsied left lung revealed that the cancer had spread to the left lung before I started the drug. That shadow now developed into small tumors in the left lung. The size of the tumor in the right lung had grown considerably.

Dr. Buroker then took me into the examination room, and after checking me and listening to my lungs, he stated, "We have to make a change to a five-hour chemotherapy of Taxol and carboplatin. You'll receive it every three weeks." He then added, "You're not going to feel very good for a few days after the chemo. You will also receive a shot of

Neulasta the day after chemotherapy. This will help prevent your white blood cell count and platelet count from dropping."

I couldn't receive the chemo that day because the insurance company had to confirm its payment. I went home and came back the next day for the five-hour treatment.

The first chemo treatment went well, and the following day I returned for the shot. That was on Thursday, and by Friday the bones in my legs, feet, and ankles hurt so badly I could hardly stand it. First I took Extra Strength Tylenol and then Aleve. When neither of those helped, I took oxycodone every five or six hours during the days when I just couldn't endure the pain any longer. After about four days the pain started letting up somewhat. Finally, on the seventh day, I began to feel stronger.

What a miserable time. I found myself thinking, *This cancer grew during the last chemo. If that's the case then this misery isn't worth it.* But later I would think *Oh, it is working because Dr. Buroker said he was sure it would reduce the tumors, that maybe even by summer I can go off of chemotherapy again like last summer, if we have good results with this treatment.*

When I went back three weeks later for lab work and to visit Dr. Buroker, I was able to report the coughing had lessened, but I didn't notice improvement in the shortness of breath. I received chemo and the shot again, as scheduled. Both Dr. Buroker and my family told me to take the pain pills more frequently. I hesitated because I thought I might have greater need of them later, but I don't need to save the pain medicine—there will always be something else that I can take. Mike told Dr. Buroker that he and Julie were going to be the "pain patrol" and make sure I took the pain medication every four hours.

Dr. Buroker then scheduled a scan for the next appointment in three weeks to be sure the chemo was making a difference. I felt like he read my mind because I was thinking, *This better be working or I am not going to continue. I feel so wretched for at least a week after the treatment. It's like the worst flu I've ever had, the most awful bone pain anyone can imagine. And then they want me to come and do it again. If the next scan reveals that the chemo is not shrinking the tumors, I am going to explain to my kids that I can't keep doing it anymore.* Yet another thought followed that one: *What if he says that the tumor hasn't grown? Is that enough reason to keep taking the chemo?*

All this indecision weighed on my mind much of the week before I went back for the scan. I believed my coughing was less frequent but wondered if that was actually true or simply my mind playing tricks on me. When I returned for lab work and the CT scan on February 4, I was concerned about what I was going to hear. Would this be the day I needed to make a decision between continuing treatment and having a better quality of life? Mike was right there beside me cheering me on, saying he knew it was going to be better.

Dr. Buroker called us into his office before I went to the examining room, which wasn't the usual routine. I thought, *Oh, no! The tumors must have grown.* Instead, Dr. Buroker was excited and wanted to show us right away that the tumors in the left lung were not visible this time, and the tumor in the right lung was half the size it was six weeks ago. I could hardly believe the news. Here I had been anticipating the possibility of stopping chemotherapy and starting hospice care. Instead, my condition had greatly improved. My heart was pounding with happiness. Mike and I both had tears of happiness in our eyes.

Sometimes my emotions dive up and down like a roller coaster. I was trying to accept the fact that I might be looking at the end of my life with no more treatments. Then my heart thumped with joy when I heard my condition improved. I was surprised at how relieved I felt. I have said since almost the beginning of my prognosis that I'm not afraid to die, and I am not. But I want to live all this life that I can. Sometimes, though, I think I don't want to live so long if I have to endure lots of pain, inability to breathe, and continual exhaustion.

Then I remember my wonderful God, who is walking every step of the way with me. My death will be as it is supposed to be. God will give me what I need when I need it—whether it is strength, trust, faith, or just the peace of knowing the journey is going as he is directing.

chapter 9

Listen to Me

When you have cancer, everyone wants to show their love and concern or to at least try to make you feel better. That is, no doubt, the reason many have said to me, "You look so good. It's hard to believe you have cancer."

I am sure I've made comments like that. I meant my words to be kind, but now that I have cancer I interpret those remarks differently. When I meet people I know at church, the store, or other places, they often tell me how great I look. Rather than feeling happy about their comment, I almost always feel a little disgruntled—even though I presume they are trying to help me feel better. Well, I may *look* good to them, but I don't *feel* good. I think to myself, *I wish*

I felt as good as you think I look. Sometimes I want to say, "If you only knew how I felt, you wouldn't say that."

Would I feel better if they said, "You look terrible," or "You don't look like you feel very well"? I don't know that I would, but just the other day when I was feeling awful from the chemotherapy, a friend said, "You look pale today." That observation helped me because I knew she had some idea of how I actually felt.

Even more than telling me I look good, there's another situation that causes me to feel even worse—when someone asks me how I'm feeling, and I choose to tell them, "I'm not doing so well today," and they still say, "But you look just great." I wonder if my honesty leads them to feel so uncomfortable that they want to avoid any conversation about my reality.

I remember in my oncology days working with a woman receiving chemotherapy. She described the day when she told a few close friends of hers that she actually dreaded losing her hair more than having the cancer itself. Her friends immediately chimed in, assuring her, "There are darling wigs out there. You'll look great." She told me, "Not a single one of *those* women was wearing a *darling wig*." She went on to explain that she would have felt much better if they had responded, "I can't imagine what it would be like to lose my hair. It must be dreadful."

That is how I feel when I mention feeling "pretty weak" or "miserable" and the response is, "Well, you look just wonderful. I would never know you had cancer if you didn't tell me." That sort of comment minimizes how unwell I am feeling. I long for people to really hear me when I say how I am. If they would respond, "I can't imagine what it is like for you to go through that," I would then feel validated. I try to remember that people have a strong desire for cancer patients to feel better. That is why they say the unhelpful and unknowingly hurtful things that they do.

I have had other experiences of being asked, "What does the doctor say about your prognosis?" When I try to be honest and tell them the doctor initially gave me a year to live, they quickly disagree with that. "Oh, you are going to be fine. What do the medical people know?" That sort of response certainly tells me they can't deal with the information I gave them. Again, it rejects my reality. I have tried to ease their obvious discomfort about my future death by saying, "Well, all of us have only today. Everyone is going to die." That eases the truth about my cancer, and they seem to feel relieved. I sometimes think, *Yes, it's true that we will all die at some point, but your death is not right in front of your nose like mine is.*

Most people are loving and kind. Even if they say hurtful things, they usually follow their thoughtless remarks by giving me a hug. That warm embrace shows more care than anything they could have said. When we are facing end-of-life issues or going through cancer of some sort, I think we are more open to receiving a gesture of love and concern than we are to words that are supposed to make us feel better.

When someone can't imagine what it is like for another person to have cancer, the best thing to do is to simply give a hug, a pat on the hand, or some other form of physical touch. Even though experts caution us about respecting people's physical space, a touch of some sort almost always feels comforting to me. It says to my heart, "I care," and "I don't know what to say, but I want you to know that I wish you did not have to experience this difficult illness."

chapter 10

Keeping My Sense of Humor

I have always used humor to cope with pain or diffi-cult situations. Laughter can certainly help at certain times. Since I was diagnosed with cancer, some of the things I laughed at aren't quite as funny as they used to be. For instance, Snickers bars have always been my favorite food. I used to say, "If I am dying and can no longer eat or drink, I want whoever is caring for me to use Snickers bars as lip balm, so I can lick my lips."

That quip seemed so funny when I would use it during presentations I gave on death and dying. Well, now that I am dealing with terminal lung cancer, that doesn't seem quite as humorous as it sounded back then. I have even kind of lost my taste for Snickers bars.

But I do still seek to cope with life by using humor. The other day I walked out of Dr. Buroker's office and the receptionist who's always there commented, "It hasn't been the best day, has it?" She must have heard that I didn't get a good report. I answered, "No. The tumor is pressing on my windpipe." She looked at me with compassion and said, "I am so sad. I love you so much." I joked, "Well, I know I will probably die trying to breathe, but it will be okay. When that time comes I will just say, 'Bring on the morphine.'" We both laughed. That was typical of my way of coping.

I'm remembering some of the times when laughter made a difference, like the time when I was working in the hospice house full-time as the director. I believed it was important to keep the spirit of the staff upbeat because taking care of dying people, going from one room to the other all day long, can be extremely stressful. The staff has little or no time to debrief. When I did full-time hospice home care, at least I had a bit of time to breathe between seeing patients. While I was driving from house to house or from one farmhouse to the other down the road or to the next small town, the miles in between allowed space for me to place the situation with that patient aside before arriving at the next one's home.

This in-between time didn't happen at the hospice residence.

One time at this hospice house, a woman's health actually improved. To her delight, she regained an ability to enjoy eating again. I brought her a tray of food and sat with her while she was eating. Suddenly she began coughing uncontrollably. I said, "I'll take the tray and bring you some food later." The woman kept coughing intensely but managed to sputter, "Leave the pie." I took the rest of the food back to the kitchen and shared that comment with the rest of the staff, who joined me in a good chuckle.

One day I visited a terminally ill African American woman in her home. I asked her about her thoughts and attitude toward what lay ahead of her. She smiled and said, "Oh, I know I am going home to Jesus. Yes, I have no doubt that I am going home. But I want you to know that I am definitely not homesick yet."

There just has to be some humor when we are dealing with end-of-life situations. Death is as normal as birth. If there can be humor with birth, why not with death? I feel that way about my own coming death too. A few weeks ago my granddaughter Margaret stayed overnight and was sleeping with me. While we were lying in bed, she turned to me and said, "I'm sorry your scan wasn't good this time, Grandma." I responded, "I'm sorry too, but that is the way things are sometimes."

She then asked, "Are you going to die?" I wanted to be honest, so I answered, "Well, yes, I am going to die someday. We all will die someday."

Margaret lay very quietly for a while. I grew concerned about what she might be thinking. Then she continued, "You know we talked about how I am coming to live with you after I graduate from high school and go to college and then work in a bank." She paused a moment and added, "Are there any banks around here that don't get robbed?" I said, "I think there are."

Margaret then asked me, "Well, what if you aren't here? What if you die before then?" I said, "I guess you will have to make other plans." She fell into deep thought for a long time and then asked, "Can I have this condo when you're gone?"

I held back a laugh and answered, "No, because I have nine grandchildren, and I couldn't give it to you." Margaret insisted, "But you *know* that I am *your favorite*." I replied, "No, Margaret. We've talked about this a lot, and I always tell you that I have nine favorite grandchildren." She wouldn't give up and persisted with, "But deep down you know that I *really am* your favorite."

I think she was more worried about her future than my dying. She is a very cute twelve-year-old who says just what she thinks. Her questions and insistence on having the condo left me smiling long after she went to sleep.

This experience with Margaret reminds me of the times of joy I've had with my other cherished grandchildren. They bring me such happiness in the midst of my cancer. When my son Joe and his twelve-year-old daughter, Anabel, came from Virginia to visit me, she brought her bubbly personality and contagious energy with her. Anabel was so happy to be here that she could hardly contain herself. Every time I would start to get up from my chair she would say, "I'll get it for you, Grammy. I'll get it. What do you need?" Then she would add, "I like taking care of you. Daddy, can I stay and take care of Grammy?"

One day we went to Gray's Lake, and Anabel pushed me in my wheelchair around the lake. She thought that was the best fun and wanted to go back to the lake the next day, but it was time for them to leave for home. She resisted leaving and begged her dad to let her stay and be my nurse. What greater gift could a grandmother with cancer receive than a twelve-year-old granddaughter wanting to be her nurse?

Garrett and George often stand by my chair and rub my head. My hair is starting to grow back. They like to feel it, and Garrett often says, "I love to feel your hair. It's so soft." I think these boys pretend that they are petting their grandma. I know it is a way for them to show me their love—at the ages of fourteen and sixteen, this can be difficult to do.

chapter 11

My Health Worsens

It is January 2016, and I have had lung cancer for two and a half years. Some days have been tolerable, but today feels like a nightmare. I was going to have a CT scan of my chest, lab work, and then receive a report about the chemo shrinking the tumors like it did last spring. As I reflect on it now, I should have been expecting something different because I was having an extremely difficult time breathing.

After I had my blood drawn, I went to radiology to have the CT scan. While waiting for the scan I was told to go have more blood drawn for a type and crossmatch because my hemoglobin was 7.8. I learned I would need a blood transfusion the next day.

I felt confident I had the answer to my increased difficulty breathing. I thought, *Oh, that is why I have had trouble. The red blood cell count is low. I must not have enough red blood cells to carry the oxygen to my lungs and body.*

When I went back to radiology to get the scan, they didn't have me scheduled for one and did not have time to do it. They sent me to the building next door to another x-ray office to have the scan. I felt vulnerable telling them, "I can't walk that far. I'm too short of breath." This meant they would have a transporter come get me with a wheelchair. I was already feeling weary when I went in to see the doctor. All that back and forth to different offices really wore me out.

After the scan, I then went to meet with Dr. Buroker, who had the results. As always, my son Mike came with me. It helps to have him there because I do not always hear clearly. When Dr. Buroker brought us into his office to look at the scan, we discovered it did not show good news. The tumors had grown significantly in both lungs. The tumor in my left lung was pressing on my trachea, causing me to have trouble getting enough breath with even the slightest activity.

This upsetting news revealed how much I had been in denial for the past several weeks. I was hardly able to walk to my kitchen, a very short distance, without becoming breathless, wheezing, and putting a lot of energy into getting enough air. Yet I hadn't acknowledged that. I kept thinking the scan would show the tumors getting smaller. It amazes me how our mind plays tricks on us, or maybe our mind does this to protect us from worry. I do know that I hadn't grasped the reality of my condition.

Dr. Buroker informed us that the current chemo could not be used anymore because the cancer had grown in spite of the Taxol and carboplatin. He then offered another one: "We have a new drug that we're having good luck with called Opdivo. We should try it."

I recognized this drug as one I saw advertised on television for squamous cell cancer. Mine was adenocarcinoma, so I mentioned that to Dr. Buroker. He replied with, "But we are having good luck with Opdivo and adenocarcinoma." I wanted to be clear about my thoughts and desires regarding any further chemo, so I clarified my wishes. "I am willing to try it because it's new," I said, "but I need to talk to you about any further treatment." I don't think Dr. Buroker liked hearing that because he then said, "There are a lot of other options out there."

I continued to explain, "I remember when I worked with you. Patients would take the best chemo first, and when the cancer had spread, they would then take the next best chemo and go on down the line until they had progressed through three or four different combinations of chemo. They would want to ward off death as long as possible. I'm not interested in doing that. I value quality of life and dying with dignity."

I added, "I have no intention of dying with chemo running into my body, trying to ward off death at all costs."

Dr. Buroker responded, "I wouldn't give you chemo that had a 10 or 15 percent chance of helping because I know you wouldn't want it."

"No," I replied, "and I wouldn't even be interested in a chemotherapy that gave a 20 or 25 percent chance. I want to live as long as I can for my family. I hate the thought of leaving them, but I am also not afraid to die. I want to be a good example to them, so they know what a *good death* is. I am at peace with my death and have a strong belief in a wonderful hereafter. I know that God is walking with me every step of the way."

Later in the day Mike asked, "Mom, why can't they do surgery and cut out that piece of cancer that's pressing on your windpipe?"

That was so like Mike, trying to find a way to help me out and give me more time. I explained surgery wouldn't help because the cancer was too extensive and already in my bloodstream. Mike then suggested, "What about radiation therapy to help shrink that area around the windpipe so you could breathe better?"

I hadn't thought of that, so I decided to ask Dr. Buroker at my next appointment. That afternoon, when I got home from the chemo treatment, I didn't want to wait that long. I went ahead and contacted Dr. Buroker to see if radiation therapy was an option. When I called, he explained, "We can't do external beam radiation, but we may be able to do a bronchoscopy and put some radium seeds down in your lung to shrink that area."

He said he would consult with Dr. Hicklin, the lung specialist, before I came in two weeks. Dr. Buroker also gave me more bad news. He didn't have the full radiology report when I was there earlier, but now he let me know two spots showed on my liver. There had never been anything there before, but I knew the developing tumors were part of having this particular type of cancer.

That night after talking to each of my three kids and bringing them up to date on the results of the scan, I read Julie's informative report about my condition on CaringBridge, a website that allows people who are seriously ill to share updates on their health. As I kept going over her post, I admitted to myself that the cancer was progressing quickly. I felt a deep sadness and cried and cried as that truth really set in. I had been in a whirlwind all day, and it took being alone and quiet to fully realize I was looking at the last part of my life. I felt overwhelmingly sad; not scared, just terribly sad. It's one thing to not be afraid of death, but it's quite another to see it coming so close.

chapter 12

What Lies Ahead for Me?

When I called Dr. Buroker last week to see if the radiation therapy would help, he assured me it would. He planned to call Dr. Hicklin to ask about the bronchoscopy and putting radium seeds into my lungs. Of course, Dr. Buroker didn't wait for this until I went to see him in two weeks but talked to Dr. Hicklin right away. Consequently, I had an appointment to see Dr. T., a physician in radiation therapy, at 8:30 a.m. the next day and then meet with Dr. Hicklin at 10:30.

I started to question if I wanted the procedure when Dr. T. explained how they would do the bronchoscopy through my nose. He would insert two wires down into my lung, and they would do a CT scan to see where the radium seeds would go. All together it would take about three hours. I asked, "Will I be asleep?" He said, "No, but you'll be drowsy." This didn't sound appealing. In fact, it frightened me and left me feeling anxious. I had never met Dr. T. before. He was pleasant but a little too "ha-ha" for me. This was one time when humor was not appropriate. He quipped some supposedly funny remark after every sentence. He had little regard for the fact that I might be dreading the procedure. His overly humorous attitude really irritated me.

After two hours with this physician, I told him I wasn't sure I wanted the procedure. His description sounded terrible. Mike felt differently and assured me, "It sounds like that bronchoscopy would really help."

I still wasn't sure when we then went to meet with Dr. Hicklin. Because I know him well, I felt a lot better talking to him. He was serious and attentive, explaining kindly that we could delay the bronchoscopy a week if I would rather wait. Dr. Hicklin could tell I was anxious about having this done. I assured him I'd go ahead with it but asked if we could do it at 1:00 p.m. because my dear friend Kathy's funeral was Wednesday morning. He agreed with the time change.

I knew I needed to go through with the procedure, even though it sounded terrible, because my family would want me to do it. But I thought to myself, *Isn't chemotherapy enough? What else is ahead?* In fact, I've been thinking since Kathy died on Friday that in some ways it would be a release to have the journey over. I know what I have ahead will be worse than what I have endured so far. I'm sure I'll have trouble breathing toward the end. That isn't going to be comfortable if I am struggling for every breath of air. That could happen or I could have a blood vessel break and rapidly hemorrhage to death.

Kathy had lung cancer and barely breathed for about fifteen hours before her death. It is so hard for families to sit and listen, to watch the labored effort to breathe and wonder when the last exhalation will happen. I hate the thought that I might do that to my family.

How is it going to be for me? Today, and for the past few days, I have been thinking of my last moments. Is the tumor going to shut off my windpipe and keep me from getting air down there? Or is my breathing just going to be extremely labored? Am I going to be in extreme pain in my chest and back? Now that the cancer has spread to my liver,

what symptoms will that bring? All those thoughts
and questions roam around in my mind these days.

How grateful I am that I have faith. I trust that
God is walking with me and will help me cope with
my journey into eternity. It must be really frightening for people who don't have God to rely on for
their strength. It's scary enough for me even with
my faith and the assurance that God is here. Still, I
ask the question, *Am I strong enough to endure what I
will have to suffer along the way?*

chapter 13

My Evolving Spirituality

Before I was diagnosed with cancer, I was busy all the time. When I was a palliative care nurse, I spent much of my life assisting people who were dying, helping them understand their terminal illness and the options open to them. I wanted each one to know they had choices they could make regarding how they spent the rest of their life with a terminal disease. I continually tried to assist them to make decisions that suited them regarding their quality of life.

I also worked with the Stephen Ministry program. This volunteer ministry included being a caregiver and paying a weekly visit to a care receiver, a person ill in body, mind, or spirit. I believe we are on this earth to help others, and this has inspired and motivated me to do this in every way I can. I've done my best to live that belief in each aspect of my adult life—not only in my work but also with my children and grandchildren. This is how I've tried to answer God's call. Because of this belief, my life usually consisted of whirlwind days.

Due to this flurry of activity, I didn't spend much time in quiet meditation. My prayer life consisted of taking part in a women's prayer group every Tuesday morning and attending Mass each Sunday. I felt I didn't need to have reflective prayer time. The constant requests and needs of those I served gave me an easy excuse to not include a space for quiet time in my daily schedule. I told myself I didn't have time to be still. I was serving God through assisting others, and that was sufficient. I never turned away anyone who asked me to help them or their friends, nor did I fail to be available to those who phoned and wanted me to listen to their problems, no matter what time of day or night.

All of that changed when I was diagnosed with stage-four lung cancer. Soon after I began receiving chemo, I was not able to continue those activities that had kept my life so full. All I could manage was to sleep and try to handle the continuous nausea.

When I was awake, I sat in my chair or on the sofa most of the time due to the extreme tiredness. I did as little as possible, not even putting much energy into eating, and I longed to have the active life I had before my lung cancer. I developed a strong yearning to visit and assist others who were ill. I felt I was failing to be a caring person.

After several months of this, and when my husband left our marriage, I found myself reading and thinking a lot. Eventually, it became clear to me that I had never really approached my spiritual life by looking deeply inside myself and by being intent on growing closer in union with God.

It was during this significant turning point that my friend happened to give me a book of daily meditations called *Jesus Calling*. This amazing book was just what I needed to open myself up to a relationship with God. Each daily reflection contains a message from Jesus spoken personally to the reader. The very first page that I read was on the morning of January 25, 2014. Jesus speaks:

> Let my love enfold you in the radiance of my glory. Sit still in the light of my presence and receive my peace. These quiet moments with me transcend time, accomplishing far more than you can imagine. Bring me the sacrifice

of your time, and watch to see how abundantly
I bless you and your loved ones.

Through the intimacy of our relationship,
you are being *transformed* from the inside out.
As you keep your focus on me, I form you into
the one I desire you to be. Your part is to yield
to my creative work in you, neither resisting it
nor trying to speed it up. Enjoy the tempo of
a God-breathed life by letting me set the pace.
Hold my hand in childlike trust, and the way
before you will open up step by step.[1]

I could hardly believe what I read. That message and many others like it sank straight into my
heart.

On another day one of the statements leaped
out at me: "These quiet moments with me transcend
time, accomplishing far more than you can imagine." Wow! That line led me to realize that I hadn't
spent much quiet time with God because I didn't
feel like I knew him. Then the message went further:
"As you keep your focus on me, I form you into the
one I desire you to be."

I thought, *I would love to be who God wants me to
be, but I have never felt I measured up.*

From then on, I started reading a meditation
from the book each day. Some days I was sure God
was looking in my window. He sure seemed to

know who I was. I decided to really try to change my prayer life and spend quiet time with Jesus to see if I could have a more personal relationship with him. This wasn't easy, even though I longed for it to happen.

I began each morning with the *Jesus Calling* daily reading. Then I spent fifteen minutes in silence listening to Jesus. Initially I had a difficult time quieting my mind—in fact, I had tried meditation earlier in my life and could never cease my thoughts. Now I wanted simply to be still and be with God, more than I ever had before.

Until I had cancer, I tried to arrange the day's time into segments of running here and there. I always had my mind on what I was doing and what came next. Now I was forced to sit in my chair due to weakness and fatigue. As I began reading daily reflections and following that with quiet time, I began to take to heart what Jesus said. Slowly, my mind became less active and this form of prayer started getting easier. I would listen to what stirred within me, and I felt like I was truly developing a personal relationship with Jesus, that he was walking with me every step of my journey. Each week it took less effort to spend twenty to thirty minutes listening to Jesus and responding to him, and I felt more at home with the love that moved in my heart.

The amazing thing that happened is that I started feeling at peace with my death. I even found myself looking forward to the love and happiness I trusted would be there for me to experience when I entered eternity with God. I found myself looking forward to seeing all those loved ones who had gone before me by their death.

Now I find the more time I spend with Jesus each morning, the more confident I am that he has my hand and will lead me home. I have no fear about dying, except for a concern about the physical pain and gasping breath I may have to experience. Even so, I know God will give me the grace and strength to deal with that when the time comes.

As I look at all of this now, I realize that if I had kept running and running, busily taking care of people in my ministry of hospice and palliative care—which I loved dearly and still truly miss—I would probably never have found this personal relationship with God. I have learned that we need to stop and be quiet, to listen and look within, in order to know who God is. I was able to see his loving presence pretty clearly in everyone else I came in contact with or cared for, but I had a difficult time thinking that this same divine presence was *within me* until I actually took the time to look and listen.

Surprising as it may sound, I am grateful for the cancer I've had during these two and a half years. Without it, I may never have taken the time to know who I really am or have been forced by physical circumstance to spend quiet time in the presence of God, to enter into the intimacy of just the two of us.

Thank you, dear Jesus, for spending time with me every morning in a very personal way. I know you have my hand in yours and you are in my heart. I love you so much.

chapter 14

My Daughter's Diagnosis

In December 2015, my condition began to deteriorate. By that time, I had been struggling with cancer for two years and six months. Julie decided to drive from Kansas City and come to my house on a Monday evening after she got off work. She arrived about 8:30 in the evening, and I immediately felt better knowing she was in my home. She always tries to take such good care of me. She fills my pantry with things from Costco like paper towels, toilet paper, and other household goods. When I was still able to drive, she would buy these items in large quantities so I didn't have to carry lots of things from the grocery store into my condo.

Julie usually takes care of the laundry and cleaning, but she mostly came this time because I was scheduled for chemo the following day and an appointment for radiation therapy two days later. We went to the chemo treatment together, and I was looking forward to shopping with her after that. I really felt pretty good that day, but I knew part of it was due to Julie's being there. When she is with me, it lifts my spirit greatly. I like it when she and her brothers come to be with me because they treat me with endearing kindness.

Ever since Mike's neck pain became much worse from a car accident last year, he has not been able to come over nearly as much. He used to bring his laptop computer and work for hours at my kitchen table. It was reassuring to have him there. Because he is able to work only about three hours a day now, it's all he can manage to come for a short period of time due to the pain draining his energy.

Julie and I have always loved being together, even during her tough high school years when we did not always see eye to eye. When she would come home from college, Gary teased the two of us. He used to say, "You two go up and sit on the bed, and I don't think either one of you takes a breath in between talking." A lot of our conversations in those days included sharing about dorm life and stories of our mutual nursing careers. Most of all, though, I think we just enjoyed being together. I've always counted that closeness as one of my greatest blessings.

While Julie and I were shopping at Kohl's, her phone rang. It was her physician in Kansas City, with the results of a CT scan she had a week or so earlier. This scan was in addition to a recent gall-bladder x-ray and in response to Julie's stomach issues from several months ago. She also had a routine colonoscopy because of family history of rectal cancer.

Those two tests turned out normal, so Julie argued with her internal medicine doctor about having the suggested CT scan of her abdomen. "I've felt perfect since the colonoscopy," she told him. "Let's skip it." He responded, "Just to not leave a stone unturned, let's have that CT scan anyhow."

Imagine Julie's shock when she answered the phone and heard her doctor say, "You have a mass on your pancreas. I want a biopsy done as soon as possible." He urged her to come back to Kansas City immediately because he wanted the biopsy done the next day.

We hurried back to my home, where Julie quickly packed. She left within an hour, and it instantly felt like all the air had been sucked out of my lungs. I kept saying to God, "How could this be happening? Anything can happen to me but please, don't let anything happen to my children."

The short amount of time Julie had been with me, from Monday at 8:30 p.m. to Tuesday at 5:00 p.m., had been filled with such enjoyment. Now I thought, *What is going to happen? How long will she live with cancer of the pancreas? I know people who have lived just a few weeks.* While my mind jumped around with these painful thoughts, Julie called me while on the road back to Kansas City. The doctor had looked at the CT scan again and noticed the tumor on the pancreas was quite localized, and he felt sure they could get it with surgery. The biopsy was scheduled for 11:00 a.m. the next day.

I have never felt so alarmed and fearful in my life. A voice deep inside of me rose up saying, *If something happens to Julie, I don't know if I can survive.*

Mike and I went to Kansas City the following day, both of us worried sick about Julie. Her physician thought her surgery would take about three hours, and we timed our trip to get to the hospital when she would be coming out of surgery. We both felt hopeful because of what the doctor said about the tumor being contained. We thought she would be all right, or at least we were telling ourselves that. I don't know if I truly believed it, but my worried mother's heart held on to that hope.

When we arrived at the hospital we found Julie's husband, Mike, sitting in the surgical waiting room. I asked, "Did the surgeon come in to talk to you?" Mike said yes, but he was reluctant to tell us the results. His hesitancy communicated a lot. My oncology nursing experience and the look on his face told me the news was not good. After we kept probing with questions, he finally acknowledged, "They opened and closed her because the liver was full of the pancreatic cancer."

My son Mike leaned against the wall and sobbed loudly. I could not believe my ears. I stood there stunned. The news was devastating. Within thirty minutes a nurse called us to Julie's room when they brought her back from recovery. Her husband, Mike, went into the room first while my son and I stayed out in the hallway. After a time the nurse came to us and said, "You can go in." We went in and walked up to Julie's bed. The fear on her face gave me chills.

Her first words to me were, "We didn't plan for this, did we?" The mother in me so wanted to hold her in my arms and rock her. She was my baby, my beloved daughter, but respecting the relationship she had with her husband I held back, knowing I could only stand there and let my heart bleed.

Julie then explained she and Mike discussed what to tell the children and decided to keep everything as positive as possible for them. My son Mike and I agreed to do it their way and assured them we would follow their wishes. Julie looked extremely tired. I asked her, "Would you like to rest for a while?" She seemed glad for the opportunity and quickly closed her eyes. Mike and I went over to the other side of her room while she and her husband shared quiet time.

After a couple of hours my son went home to get Julie's children. I stayed at the hospital with Julie and my son-in-law. When Mike got back we went out into the hallway, while they told the children about her surgery.

Julie received numerous phone calls and several visitors throughout the evening. Later that evening, my son Mike and I took the children home, while my son-in-law Mike stayed all night with Julie. I longed to spend the night with her, but I knew it was not my place. I hugged her tightly as I left and could feel the love in her responding embrace.

chapter 15

My Loneliness

It is now the end of January 2016. As the cancer progresses, so does my sense of isolation. I am homebound now, and there is no one else with terminal lung cancer that I can easily talk to. This loneliness feels like a big rock on my chest. It sits there and reminds me every day of its presence. But I also experience loneliness as empty space, a hollow nothingness.

People come to visit and try to understand. They tell me how I'm feeling, when they really have no idea what I am experiencing. I try to be a good listener because I know they are sincerely trying to comprehend the situation. I appreciate that. But I am left alone with how it actually is to have cancer. The loneliness fills my entire being. It is with me every moment of my waking hours. But I put my hand in God's hand and know deep down I am not alone. God is walking with me every step of the way.

There is also the matter of living alone. Sometimes the solitude is comforting. At other times, like when Mike is here, I'm grateful to have the company. Then there are situations when people come to visit that my mind is so full of my own pain it is difficult to entertain or receive them. This tension between desiring solitude and feeling lonely comes and goes. It is stronger some days than others.

Just this morning my prayer group came to my home at 7:00 a.m. as they do every Tuesday. Our gathering was such a spiritual time. We prayed, laughed together, and truly felt like sisters of the Spirit. I didn't feel the least bit lonely while they were here, and I felt loved. I realized then there are times in my life when I don't feel isolated by this cancer, but I tend to forget that when loneliness takes over.

Another part of my loneliness includes the fact that I am the only living member of my immediate family. My mother died when I was forty-four. My father took his last breath in my home the week before his ninetieth birthday. My twin brother, Joe, was killed in an automobile accident at the age of twenty-two. My oldest brother, Ed, succumbed to a neuromuscular disease sixteen years ago, and my next oldest sibling, Rich, died of lung cancer metastasized to the brain. My brother Gene died about six years later. I still remember standing at the gravesite of my youngest brother's burial and thinking, *I am the only one left.* I frequently experience this stark emptiness of having none of my family of origin with me now.

My dear husband Gary died in 1994. I did not know if I could survive the grief that overtook me with his death. He had been my husband for thirty-two years, and because his health was compromised for much of that time, he became the focus of my life. I felt like half my heart went with him when he died. The void was unbelievable. Every time one of my family members died, it felt like Gary died again. As my cancer has progressed, I find myself yearning to be reunited with him and all my relatives.

My belief that Gary and the members of my family are waiting for me really helps me cope with my loneliness because I know I am going to be with them. I often speak to them and say, "Mom and Dad, Ed, Rich, Joe, and Gene, I am going to be with you again." Then I sit here and think about each one and the special memories I associate with them. When I think about my Gary, I can't wait to go home.

In spite of this way of coping with my loneliness, I still feel the intensity of it every time I think of leaving my children, their spouses, and my grandchildren. I love having them come to visit. When they do I forget my isolation for a while. But I feel it again when they leave. It seems unbearable to consider parting from my family, especially the grandchildren before they become adults.

In November 2014, my granddaughter Ruby was diagnosed with a rare blood disease and underwent a bone marrow transplant on the East Coast. I yearned to be with her, but my cancer tied me close to home. I felt lonely for Ruby, wanting to hold her and assure her of my love.

The thought of leaving my dear daughter, Julie, when she is going through the most trying time of her life, breaks my heart. As I write this, Julie has begun receiving an intensive chemotherapy that is as tough as my initial treatment. How I long to be there with her. There is no end to loneliness with this cancer.

Editor's note: Julie has continued to respond to her own cancer diagnosis with hope. In July 2016, she underwent surgery to remove her spleen and the tumor in her pancreas, and as of August 2016, she is on a regimen of chemotherapy.

chapter 16

My Final Chapter

This will be the last chapter that I will write. On March 14, I had a CT scan, and when Dr. Buroker came in after the CT scan, he told us the tumors in my lungs and liver were much worse. That news did not surprise me because I had had difficulty breathing for the past several days. Any movement was challenging, and even walking into the bathroom caused severe shortness of breath. My breathing sometimes consisted of gasps, even when I wasn't moving my body. When Julie came to be with me the past weekend, my difficulty with breathing concerned her. Mike, on the other hand, has a tendency to deny things and said, "I don't think her breathing has changed much." Yet I could hardly get enough air after just walking a few steps.

When Dr. Buroker broke the news about how much the tumors had grown, I knew instantly my journey with cancer was now hastening toward death. Mike recognized this too and started crying. Dr. Buroker spoke gently to me: "There is no more chemo that would be of benefit to you. But you know we'll do all we can to keep you comfortable." When he said that, I thought of how often I had said those very same words to cancer patients when they could no longer receive chemo.

Dr. Buroker ordered liquid morphine for the intense pain in my ribs and to lessen the air hunger. I returned home that day facing the truth of my impending death. I knew it was time for me to enter hospice care in my home. My children and I had conversations in the past about how this could be possible. The condo has three bedrooms. There was plenty of room for a hospital bed in the living room and space for someone to stay with me overnight. When the children came, they could stay there with me.

I have mixed feelings about being in hospice care. It is the turning point for me, the movement toward death. Until now I have been trying to stay alive for the sake of the children. In a way, I feel relief knowing I do not have to fight this anymore. I've completed the journey. Now I wait.

Four days later, I gave up a huge piece of my independence by not being able to go to the bathroom by myself. In my weakened condition I had to start using the commode full-time. This might not seem like a big issue to some people, but it felt highly important to me. I compare it to giving up my driver's license some months ago, which I felt was a huge loss at the time. But the big difference between using a commode full-time and losing my driver's license is the loss of dignity that goes with using the commode. With the loss of my driver's license, I was still able to have someone give me a ride without embarrassment or a cost to my privacy. Using a commode and having someone empty it— that is something I did not even want to imagine. And yet, it is my new reality. Dr. Buroker said Monday that I may have one, two, or three months to live. If I can never go to the bathroom alone—what a depressing thought. As I used the commode yesterday, I sat and cried, thinking about never being able to have the independence and privacy of the bathroom again.

Using the commode was not only difficult for me. It was even more so for Mike. He told me that the day he walked into my home and realized I could no longer walk to the bathroom he thought, *No, I can't! I can't help my mother get on and off the commode. I can't wipe her. I can't do it.* But right after that thought came another: *I can. Yes, I can. Without any questions asked.* When he told me that later on, I was deeply touched by the unselfish, generous heart he has. Since then Mike has stayed every night with me and has been a tremendous help caring for me, especially when I wake and cannot breathe.

So much changes for me each day. After the hospital bed was delivered to my house, I held off using it for as long as I could. Being in the hospital bed symbolized getting closer to the end. I found myself continuing to sit and sleep in my easy chair but finally had to surrender and move to the hospital bed. All this reminds me that it just takes time to adjust and give up what cannot be kept, no matter how much I desire it to be otherwise.

Because I am more vulnerable and dependent, I am especially grateful for those who provide me with opportunities to have as much control over my life as possible. Being asked what I might need instead of being told what someone thinks I need means a lot to me. "Would you like to have your water refreshed? Do you need some lip balm? Can I make some lunch for you? Do you want your pillow moved?" Talking directly to me instead of whispering to another person in the room about my condition also adds to my sense of dignity and self-worth.

The other day some friends brought lunch. I felt strong enough to be able to sit at the table. I wanted to use my walker to get to the table. They immediately tried to put me in a chair and push it over to the table, but I asked them to let me do it myself. It took quite a bit of time and effort for me to walk the few feet to the table, but I felt good doing it on my own. These small but important efforts of mine mean a lot to me.

It's also helpful to me when people who are present do not insist I eat more than I am able. I eat small portions of food now, and that is okay. I remember when my mother was dying, I kept trying to get her to take one more bite of food. Finally, she told me, "I didn't eat much, but I feel like I've had a Thanksgiving dinner with every bite. I've eaten all my life for you kids. Let me be." Now I understand what she meant because I feel the same way when people urge me to eat more than I can.

With death coming closer, each night I wonder, *Is this my last night?* I find myself asking that sort of question even about simple things such as, *Is this my last bowl of potato soup?* I know there will be a last time to meet with my book club and my Tuesday morning prayer group. Time is elusive, and I have only so much time on earth left.

One of the areas that created such sadness in me came recently when I realized I had to limit my visitors. I just don't have energy to have many people come each day. I have always loved people and valued my time with both friends and colleagues. Since receiving Dr. Buroker's prediction that I have only a short time left, my phone rarely stops ringing and people constantly stop by. One day I said out loud, "I can't breathe physically, and I feel just as crowded mentally. I have to have some space to be quiet and tend to my dying process." Yet when I made the decision to have fewer visitors, I felt such a loss, as if it was a betrayal of those who care about me. Still, I know I can no longer have so much activity if I am going to remain peaceful and be prepared for my remaining days.

Not all the transitions in these last three weeks have been difficult and challenging. Some changes feel like a blessing. This is especially so in the area of my interior life. My spirituality has definitely changed. Since I am now directly facing my death, I feel much more peaceful. During this time with cancer, I have spent more time at the feet of Jesus. I used to believe that my actions were what counted the most, but now I know without a doubt that my relationship with God is the most important part of my life's journey.

People have asked me, "What gives you hope now that you know you are facing death?" I tell them the time I am spending with God brings me immense hope. I trust how much God loves me. Since being diagnosed with lung cancer, my quiet meditation has convinced me of that and strengthened my faith. I spend time each day meditating on God in my life. That prayer time has enriched my relationship with him significantly. My greatest comfort comes from growth in the depth of my relationship with God since I started this journey with cancer over two and a half years ago.

I trust where I am going and what the future will hold. I know none of us are perfect as we face the end of our lives. When death arrives, all I can offer to God is the best I have done.

I have hope and feel relief in my God, who is walking beside me every step of the journey, assuring me I am on the right path, that this is the one I am meant to be on. I take much comfort in my deep belief in God and feel that I have done the best I could do all my life. Each morning when I wake up, I continue to choose to give my love to others. Every day, through my love of God, I continue to do this in my prayer and the way I love those who visit and take care of me.

One of the biggest challenges of this final journey is the thought of leaving my children and grandchildren behind. This pain seldom eases. At the same time, I have had some comforting moments when I think about them and what I want them to remember. I wrote letters to be given to each of them after I am gone. The other day, when I reread the letters I wrote to each of them, I felt they were here beside me. How dear they are to me.

I often sense the presence of my wonderful husband Gary, and it is a strength and comfort. One morning, when my prayer group came to pray with me, they stood around my chair and blessed me. Later, one of the women told me she saw the blurred figure of a man standing nearby when I was being blessed. What joy I felt sensing it was Gary, that he is here with me waiting to welcome me with open arms. Last night I dreamed I died and was on my way to heaven. I was traveling up and felt such love and peace.

During this final part of my life, I sometimes question myself and wonder if I am doing it right. By that I mean, "Am I living my life to the fullest, showing God the best I can to everyone I come in contact with?" It is my hope to have been forgiven fully by those I have hurt in any way, especially those I am unaware of whom I might have harmed. I want my death to touch those I love in a positive way. I long for them to find joy in the things we have shared, to look back with a smile and not a tear. I hope they will think of something I have said and then chuckle.

Even here, so close to the end of my life, I still find things that bring laughter. Just the other day, I was talking with a friend about my funeral and mentioned I'd like to have "the washing of the feet" as Jesus did at the Last Supper. For me, that action symbolizes the service I tried to provide to others through my life. When Fr. Michael Amadeo came to visit recently, my friend and I suggested this be part of the service. We discussed the possibility, and when Fr. Michael left, we continued the conversation about how he could facilitate the washing and incorporate it into his homily. Then we both started to laugh when my friend said, "Here we are, writing Fr. Michael's homily for him."

One would think that the dying process is difficult, but I am finding it easier than I imagined. I know everyone's experience of death is theirs alone. For me, it is more peaceful than I ever thought it would be. I have no fear of death. I thank God for this every single day.

If I were to summarize my life, I'd put it this way: I have loved people so much. I have always tried to serve others by how I cared for them. This approach has felt right, normal, and spontaneous. I still try to maintain that approach each day in this final part of my life. People are incredible human beings in how they respond to our love. I want to share as much love with them as possible.

This final chapter reaches its conclusion, as does the last chapter of my life. As I take my leave, I trust that God continues to walk with me every step of the way.

Afterword
by Joyce Rupp

Joyce Hutchison took her final breath on May 7, 2016, almost three years after being stunned by the diagnosis of lung cancer.

Two months before her death, Joyce's weakened body would not allow her hands strength enough to write, so she dictated the last chapter of this book. We often went over the previous chapters, honing them until she felt satisfied with the content. Knowing others might benefit from reading her book gave Joyce significant pleasure. She felt this was one last service she could give others. The desire to contribute generously never left her.

On my last visit, Joyce still had strength enough to carry on short pieces of conversation. At first she drifted in and out of alertness. At one point Joyce opened her eyes and questioned, "I wonder if I'm ready. Am I ready?" Long pause, eyes half closed. Eventually, I asked, "What would you need in order to be ready?" She surprised me with an immediate response: "What if it's the moment of my death, and I panic, and I don't have a glass of water?" Another long pause with her eyes shut, then open.

I wanted Joyce to know I heard whatever concerned her, so I continued, "A glass of water. What would you want that for?" To which she simply answered, "To give it. To have it ready."

There it is, I thought. *Joyce still has that amazing concern for others.* I thought immediately of the gospel verse, "Whoever gives even a cup of cold water to one of these little ones . . . truly I tell you, none of these will lose their reward" (Mt 10:42, NRSV). Joyce often remarked that she tried to care for others as if she were tending to Jesus. As she lay dying she still wanted to "give a cup of water."

Joyce planned her vigil (wake) and funeral Mass a few months before her death. She explained to those of us who helped her with the preparation, "I want the focus to be about giving of ourselves. I hope the services will be about love."

The central aspect of the evening vigil included a foot washing, which Joyce thought would express an attitude of humble, compassionate care. When she laid out her plans, she commented that she continually approached nursing, hospice, and Stephen Ministry with the understanding that she was a "foot washer," privileged to be of service. Those who knew Joyce were aware of her open, lavish heart and how humbly she approached the good she did for others. Having this as part of the vigil made a loud and clear statement about Joyce's life and encouraged others to live in a similar manner.

Her attitude of humility is reflected in this writing from Caryll Houselander's *The Reed of God*:

> We could scrub the floor for a tired friend, or dress a wound for a patient in a hospital, or lay the table and wash up for the family; but we shall not do it in martyr spirit or with that worse spirit of self-congratulation, of feeling that we are making *ourselves* more perfect, more unselfish, more positively kind.
>
> We shall do it just for one thing, that our hands make Christ's hands in our life, that our service may let Christ serve through us, that our patience may bring Christ's patience back to the world.[1]

Once Joyce finished her book and completed the task of planning the vigil and funeral liturgy, there was little left for her to do. She now gave what energy she had to the effort of dying. She mentioned more than once that she wanted to "die a good death" and that she didn't know why it was taking so long.

As we neared the end of our final conversation, Joyce reached over for her basket holding the book *Jesus Calling*. She pulled it onto her lap, looked up, and said in a concerned voice, "I haven't done any reading lately." To which I responded, "Joyce, you have done your reading. You are prepared. You are ready when the call comes."

Joyce objected, "I sleep so much. I don't do anything." I encouraged her, "You have arrived at the place of just being. Remember the huge change you've made from giving to receiving. All you need is to let yourself go when the moment of death comes and slip into the arms of God."

My dying friend looked at me with the trust of a young child and asked, "Do you think that is how it will be?" I realized in that moment my arrogance in telling someone else what it is like to die, when I had not done so myself. I looked at her with a smile and said, "I don't know. I've not experienced dying. But I think that is how it will be for you. You and I both know from others who have died that surrender is always required. Give yourself over to God and let it happen."

With a strong voice, Joyce said, "That sounds good." She then reminded me, as she had done numerous times before, how much she was looking forward to those who were waiting for her. Because she had accompanied so many of the dying in their final stage of illness, she often commented with a laugh, "I know more people in heaven than I do here on earth."

On May 7, there must have been a huge throng of light-filled beings who came toward Joyce, with their loving arms outstretched, to welcome her home.

Joyce Hutchison (1940–2016) was Iowa's first hospice nurse and an expert on care of the dying. Hutchison served as palliative care coordinator and hospice educator for Iowa Health Hospice and Home Care in Des Moines. A registered nurse, her clinical experience included work as an oncology nurse, home care nurse, and residence team director of a hospice facility. A member of the National Hospice and Palliative Care Organization and the Oncology Nursing Society, she also frequently presented workshops on care of the dying and hospice.

She was the coauthor, with Joyce Rupp, of two best-selling books, *May I Walk You Home?* and *Now That You've Gone Home*. She was the mother of three and grandmother of nine.

Notes

Foreword

1. Neale Donald Walsch, *Home with God: In a Life That Never Ends* (New York: Atria Books, 2006), vii.

6. Preparing for My Journey

1. Sarah Young, *Jesus Calling: Enjoying Peace in His Presence* (Nashville: Thomas Nelson, 2004), 72.

13. My Evolving Spirituality

1. Sarah Young, *Jesus Calling: Enjoying Peace in His Presence* (Nashville: Thomas Nelson, 2004), 26.

Afterword

1. Caryll Houselander, *The Reed of God: A New Edition of a Spiritual Classic* (Notre Dame, IN: Christian Classics, 2006), 59.